KEIGHLEY
A Pictorial History

The view from Parkwood district looking north west across the centre of Keighley, 1950. This was before the new town centre was built and there were still some mill chimneys across the landscape.

KEIGHLEY
A Pictorial History

J. Stewart Cardwell

Phillimore

1997

Published by
PHILLIMORE & CO. LTD.
Shopwyke Manor Barn, Chichester, West Sussex

ISBN 1 86077 062 2

Printed and bound in Great Britain by
BIDDLES LTD.
Guildford, Surrey

List of Illustrations

Frontispiece: The view from Parkwood district looking north west

Acknowledgements

Most of the photographs are taken from the Keighley and District Photographic Society's survey collection and numbers 7, 41, 45, 63, 64, 66, 105, 107, 133, 137 and 151 are from the author's own collection of photographs, both of which are housed in the Keighley Reference Library. Numbers 58 and 104 are reproduced by courtesy of the *Keighley News* and no.124 by courtesy of Keith Howarth, A.I.B.P. The author would like to thank Carole Buckley, for giving her permission to use numbers 6, 81 and 112, which were taken by Harold Horsman, A.R.P.S., her late father, who spent a great deal of time recording old Keighley on film.

The author would like to thank Dr. Ian Dewhirst, John Triffitt, Judi Unwin and my wife, Irene, for their help and encouragement. I would also like to thank Fred Gettings for his help in reproducing the illustrations and Kevin Seaton and my wife for the use of their postcard collections.

Introduction

Keighley is a town of some 60,000 population, which is situated 400 feet above sea level, at the point where the river Worth joins the river Aire. To the north are the Yorkshire Dales and two miles to the south west is the village of Haworth, where the Brontë sisters lived at the parsonage with their father and wrote novels about the area. The town's situation between two rivers made it an ideal location, during the industrial revolution, as they supplied the power for the textile machinery and water for washing the wool.

The early history of Keighley is very sketchy and the first records of habitation are to be found on the moors around the area, which are littered with tools belonging to prehistoric flint workers. Bronze-and Iron-Age man left earthworks and stone circles, along with a number of cup and ring stones, which had a religious significance. There are no Roman remains in Keighley, apart from a Roman road which may have crossed Airedale to the south east of Keighley, at West Morton, on its way from Manchester to Ilkley.

The first record of a settlement appears in Domesday Book in 1086, when it was spelt Chichleai. The general consensus appears to be that the name was derived from a Saxon named Cyhha, who cultivated a clearing in the extensive forests which abounded in the Aire Valley at that time, but there are no records of his existence. The spelling has had many changes including Kichalaie, Kykelei, Kygheley, Kithelai, Keghelay, Kighley and Keighley. The other problem is how to pronounce the name. Even to this day, it is pronounced by most visitors to the town as 'Keeley', whereas the correct pronunciation is 'Keathley'.

The date of the first parish church is rather obscure but appears to be between 1100 and 1245, as William Le Vavasour was appointed as the first rector in the latter year. A stone was found in the old steeple with the figures 1111 inscribed upon it, but there is some doubt as to whether or not this was a date.

Keighley was granted a market charter in 1305, and 'Henry Kighley procured from Edward the First, for this his manor, the privileges of a Market, a Fair, and Free Warren, so that none might enter these grounds to chase therein, ... without the permission and leave of the said Henry and his successors'. The old fair was held on 27 October of each year but was later altered to 8 November and then to 8 May. The market was on Church Green until November 1833, when it was moved to the site of the new covered market, in Low Street, which was built in 1971.

The events of the reformation in the 16th century passed Keighley by, almost unnoticed, apart from nearby Bolton Abbey. This Augustinian priory, which is about eight miles from Keighley on the banks of the river Wharfe, was rased to the ground by Henry VIII in 1542. The confiscated property and Bolton Hall was bestowed on the Earl of Cumberland for about £2,500.

The town went about its daily life in comparative obscurity until the time of the Civil War, when at the end of 1644, 'a party of about 150 horse from Skipton, taking advantage of the absence of Col. Brandling, who commanded, fell suddenly upon the Parliamentary quarters at Keighley, where they surprised the guards, got into the town, and took near a hundred prisoners, sixty horse and other booty'. These were later recovered by a Col. Lambert and his party, killing 15 and taking 20 prisoners. Other skirmishes took place and reference to them can be found in the parish registers, including two soldiers buried in 1643 and a soldier of Colonel Cromwell's regiment buried 1644. Another possible reference to the Civil War is the district of Guardhouse which is in an elevated position above the town, making it an ideal position to defend, where buildings were probably used to house a Parliamentary garrison.

In 1672, the Nonconformist preacher, the Rev. Oliver Haywood, who often visited Keighley, said it was a 'barren place for religion' and Rev. Miles Gale, Rector of Keighley, confirmed this at the start of the 18th century, when he said that there was 'only one dissenting place of worship in the town and that was occupied by the Society of Friends'. The Friends or Quakers were established in Keighley within a few years of their beginnings nationally, which was probably in the late 1640s, although a precise date is not known. They were a minority religion in Keighley and this can be gleaned from their registers, which start in 1654 and end about 1760 and contain the following records: 148 births, 48 marriages and 171 deaths. They also contain many references to their suffering for their beliefs:

> In the year 1660, a number of Friends being met together ... at Laycock near Keighley, the constable of Keighley sent a company of rude men with club bill and staves, who did violently pull Joseph Jescrop and William Clayton out of the meeting, with twenty more, and carried them before Charles Fairfax of Menston, called a Justice, who tendered them the oath of allegiance which for conscience' sake and in obedience to the commands of Christ they would not take, and so they were committed by him to the Castle of York, where they remained six weeks and were then released by the Judge.

The Friends' Meeting House was built in Mill Street in 1690 but was later moved to Skipton Road and still remains there to this day.

In 1742 John Nelson, the pioneer of Methodism in Yorkshire, was invited to preach a sermon at John Wilkinson's house, a journeyman shoemaker. He preached to some of the neighbours and afterwards a small class was formed, which met regularly and at the end of each meeting, Mr. Wilkinson read a prayer and pronounced the benediction. This was the start of Methodism in Keighley. In 1746, John Wesley visited Keighley and 'preached in a yard'. He returned on 13 occasions and preached to an ever increasing flock. The first Methodist chapel was built by subscription on Temple Row in 1754, on a piece of ground which was part of an orchard. Soon this property was too small for the growing congregation and so the chapel was enlarged in 1777, with new galleries. On 28 July 1845 the foundation stone for Temple Street Chapel was laid and it was opened the following year, using the old chapel as a Sunday School. As congregations diminished, the chapel was no longer required and it is now converted into a mosque and the old Sunday School is now used as a plumber's merchants.

The Wesleyan Society was started by John Laycock, of Upper Green at Ingrow, in 1765 and by 1777, had 20 members. These classes expanded and spread to various locations, usually in people's houses. By 1860 it had become necessary to make changes, as all the properties were being filled and it was decided to build a new chapel and schools, with a schoolhouse for the teacher. The schools and house were opened in 1862, the corner stone for the chapel was laid by Sir Isaac Holden and the inaugural services were held in April 1864. Unfortunately, in May 1865, the foundation stones at the front of the chapel gave way, because of tunnelling for the Worth Valley railway. The chapel had to be rebuilt, using the same stone, and this was opened two years later.

The Baptist church in Keighley started in a small way, meeting at various houses, like the Wesleyans, and up to 1860 the main building was in Turkey Street. In that year a building fund was set up and later a site was acquired from the Duke of Devonshire. In July 1863 the foundation stone was laid for Albert Street Baptist Chapel and it was opened for worship in September 1865.

In 1695 the population of Keighley was 1,704, including 112 freeholders in 100 dwellings, when some form of census was taken. This was recorded in the diary of the Rev. Miles Gale, who also states that, 'the poor of the parish are numerous, and maintained by assessment, which sometimes amounts to £140 a year, besides many private gifts'. Paupers in the town were helped mainly by the poor rate, which was levied on householders by the Overseers of the Poor. There was a workhouse some distance from the centre of town, at Exley Head; but the majority of relief took the form of help to individuals, to help them survive, usually in the form of clothing or rent. The 1834 Poor Law Amendment Act was introduced and, after opposition in the town, the Keighley Union was formed. A new and much larger workhouse was built in Oakworth Road, in 1858, much nearer the centre of town. This was converted into a home for the elderly about 1950 but is now used as part of Keighley College. The old workhouse, which was no more than a large farmhouse, was closed in 1860, as it was too small and unfit for human habitation.

During the 16th and 17th centuries, the wool textile trade was expanding into quite a large cottage industry in the Keighley area, using water from the local streams and thin seams of coal, which could be found in the hills around the town. There is evidence of this from the parish registers, which include entries such as: 'John Hartley, a clothier, buried 29th. December, 1577'.

By the start of the 18th century, the woollen trade had given way to worsted manufacture and the introduction of machinery. The first worsted mills in Keighley were built in about 1808 and these included Aireworth Mill and Wire Mill at Ingrow. In 1779 there had been trouble in the Lancashire textile towns, caused by the development of factories for spinning cotton as opposed to domestic cotton spinning. Birkacres Mill in Chorley was burnt to the ground during a riot and the owners decided that Keighley was the ideal location to rebuild their business. The town had good communications with Lancashire, an excellent water supply and no trouble with the local population. There had been a slump in the wool trade in the town and so this made way for the first cotton mill in Yorkshire, which commenced production on 30 June 1780. This was Low Mill, started by Ramsdens of Halifax and bought by the Lancashire cotton spinners, Clayton and Walsham, to replace the mill at Chorley. The machinery was made under the direction of Sir Richard Arkwright and eventually the mill became the property of J. and J. Craven. This produced speculation in the cotton trade and by 1805, there were 10 cotton mills in the Keighley area. With the increase in the textile industry, the population of the parish rose accordingly:

```
1801    5,745
1821    9,223
1841   13,378
1861   21,859
1881   33,540
```

By the middle of the 19th century, the worsted industry was making a comeback and by 1858 there were about thirty mills and several weaving sheds in the parish. This trend continued until the middle of this century, when cheap imports destroyed the local textile trade.

Along with textiles, Keighley also made the machinery for the mills in the area and soon these firms were used throughout the world. A local man, Richard Hattersley, in 1789 started producing rollers, spindles and flyers and eventually went on to produce looms. A short time later, William Smith founded the firm of Prince-Smith and Stells, who made spinning frames. Towards the end of the 19th century, other firms followed and soon Keighley had quite a reputation for engineering as well as textiles. By the 1980s most of these companies had gone the same way as the textile industry and now the town's engineering skills are limited to two or three large firms, which make products as diverse as escalators, lifts and precision tools.

The original parish church survived until 1805 and was essentially the same building on the outside as the one first built on the site, although it had seen changes in interior detail. It was re-seated in 1703 and re-windowed in 1710 by the rector Miles Gale (1680-1720) and was restored again in 1770. Because of the rapid rise in population, the small old church had to be rebuilt in 1805, to cope with the increase in the number of parishioners. Unfortunately, the roof was made of poor materials and by 1840 it was decided that the church must be substantially rebuilt again. It was not until 24 February 1846 that the foundation stone for the present building was laid and it was consecrated by Thomas, Bishop of Ripon, in 1848. The church was built at a cost of nearly £7,000 and was in the Perpendicular style. At the time the parish church was being rebuilt, as a sign of prosperity in the town, other daughter churches were being opened, including St John's Ingrow in 1843, Christ Church Oakworth in 1846 and St Mary's Eastwood in 1855. In recent years, because of falling attendances, it was decided to use the parish church for Non-conformist services as well as Anglican, and so Methodists also use the building and it has now been re-named the Shared Church.

Up to about 1700 the pack-horse was the only major form of transport and the roads were totally inadequate for anything more sophisticated. In 1735 the Keighley and Kendal Turnpike Trust was appointed and an Act for repairing and widening the road was passed. Other roads followed and soon a network of improved roads existed, which was financed by tolls imposed by the trusts. When the Thackley to Skipton section of the Leeds and Liverpool Canal was opened on 21 March 1774, this made Keighley an important town in the Aire Gap through the Pennines. The 19th century saw the introduction of the railway to the area and in 1847 the Leeds and Bradford extension of the Midland Railway was opened in Keighley, which eventually joined the East Lancashire line at Colne. In 1867, the Worth Valley Railway opened its line from Oxenhope to join the Midland Railway at Keighley and improve communications between Oxenhope, Haworth, Oakworth and Keighley. This helped the mills in the Worth Valley to prosper and as Keighley eventually linked up with Halifax, with the opening of the Great Northern line, in 1884, it improved trade with other parts of

Yorkshire. The Worth Valley line is now a major tourist attraction, organised by its preservation society, which runs steam trains up to Oxenhope.

Keighley's original station was built in 1846 behind Cavendish Street and both lines crossed Bradford Road by means of a level crossing. This created problems as the road traffic increased and it was decided to build a bridge over the railway. After a great deal of discussion, which lasted 10 years, Station Bridge was opened in 1879. It was also decided to build a new station on Bradford Road to replace the old one and this was opened in 1883. During the second half of the 20th century, the rail service declined with the increasing use of the motor car. It was in 1968 that Keighley had a fight on its hands to retain its station. Fortunately, the station was not closed and rail service has made a slight comeback, with the introduction of electrification. The 19th century was also the time of the tram and in 1889 the first horse-drawn trams were seen on the streets of Keighley, but it was not until 1904 that the routes were electrified. In 1924, the council had a problem financing the tracks which needed replacing and eventually decided on a trackless system and was the first town to do this. Keighley were also pioneers in the development of motor bus services and introduced their first bus service between Utley and Eastburn in April 1913. By 1932, the corporation was competing with other transport companies and was finding it increasingly difficult to continue on its own. Its main rival was the West Yorkshire Company, with which it eventually combined, for local services, to become Keighley-West Yorkshire Services. This continued for a number of years, but the service is now provided locally by Keighley and District Travel Limited.

One of the earlier forms of local government in Keighley was the Water Works Company, which was able to supply water to certain areas of the town. As its powers were limited, the Improvement Commissioners were granted powers in 1824 by Act of Parliament, and the Local Board of Health, who replaced them, was constituted in 1855. This body was able to supply the town with sewers, pavements, pure water and a gas works. Unfortunately there were complaints about the size of the rates, which had risen from 1s. 6d. in the pound in 1855 to 3s. 3d. in 1879. For some time it was considered that the Local Board was not efficient and its powers were limited. An attempt was made as early as 1867 to give the town a higher status. It was not until July 1882 that Keighley's Charter of Incorporation was granted and an area identical with the Local Board's, became the new borough. This boundary was limited to one mile from the centre of the town but was extended in 1895 and again in 1938. Since 1974, Keighley has become four of the electoral wards in Bradford Metropolitan Council.

On introducing the first mayor of Keighley, in 1882, the acting mayor, Mr. John Brigg, who took on the office before the appointment of the first town council, recalled changes which had taken place in the town:

> I remember perfectly, the time when the self-elected Improvements Commissioners held sway, when three constables or watchmen used to patrol the streets calling out the time of the night and the state of the weather. I was standing on the causeway of Mr. Laycock's shop when the first mail coach came up to the Devonshire Arms [now the *Grinning Rat*] and although I cannot remember the first introduction of gas, I well remember hearing my father relate the struggles which took place at the Commissioner's meetings before the 'nasty dangerous compound' was adopted for lighting purposes.

Secondary education in Keighley goes back to 1713, when John Drake left a yearly salary for the master of the school in his will and on 26 August 1716 the corner stones were laid for the Grammar School in Cooke Lane. He was buried in the parish church and his epitaph is still to be seen:

> Here lies the body of John Drake,
> Who never did his friends foresake;
> Houses and lands he left to be
> A Free School Master's salary;
> He lived and died without a mate,
> And yealded to the laws of fate.

The school continued until 1854, when a new building opened. In 1872, it was found that the Grammar School for Boys and the Mechanics' Institute were duplicating each other's work. These were combined to become the Trade School and the School for Science and Art, later to be known as the Boys' Grammar School. The girls' school, called Drake and Tonson, was opened in 1872 and was used until the present school, Greenhead Grammar School, was erected in 1933. The Boys' Grammar School moved to the site of Oakbank House, the home of the Haggas family, in 1964. It was renamed Oakbank Grammar School but the 'Grammar' was later dropped, and both schools are now co-educational comprehensive.

The general education of the town began in 1825, when John Farrish, John Bradley and William Dixon met to consider forming 'a society for mutual instruction, and establishing a library for the same'. On 14 February 1825, the society was established and the first public meeting was held in the National School room, at Mill Hill. The entrance fee was 5s. and the weekly subscription was 2d. It was essential from the start that they had a large room and so meetings were held in the Free Grammar School in Cooke Lane. This was the start of the Mechanics' Institute, which was one of the earliest in the country. In 1835, a new building was opened in North Street, as large meetings were now held in various locations in the town, such as the Court House, Wesleyan school room and Keighley Savings banks and this would bring them under one roof. The Institute continued to go from strength to strength and by 1858, there were 180 students, 358 members and almost 300 books in the library. In 1864, it was decided to form a committee 'to consider the best means to build a New Mechanics Institution', as the present accommodation was becoming inadequate. The foundation stone was laid on 12 December 1868 by Mr. Isaac Holden and the new building in Cavendish Street was declared open by the Duke of Devonshire on 30 September 1870. Unfortunately this fine building was burnt down in March 1962 and remained a ruin until 1967, when it was replaced with a modern technical college extension.

Cliffe Castle was the home of Henry Isaac Butterfield, a member of the wealthy Butterfield family, who ran an extremely lucrative textile firm, Butterfield Brothers. This house replaced a mansion known as Cliffe Hall, which in turn was an enlargement of a much smaller residence called Netherwood House. The cost of laying out the 300 acres of land and the building of the house in the castellated style was estimated at £130,000 and justified the name of 'castle'. In 1949, the castle was bought by Sir Bracewell Smith for the use of the people of Keighley. After considerable alterations and repairs, due to dry rot, it now houses the town's museum. In 1819, William Sugden, another wealthy textile manufacturer, built Eastwood House, which stayed in the hands of the Sugden family until 1888. When the then owner of the house, John G. Sugden, died, the house came on the market and was sold but was eventually bought by public subscription and became the property of the town council. Towards the end of the 19th century, the Keighley Scientific and Literary Society housed a collection of minerals and geological specimens in the Mechanics' Institute and later a natural history collection was bought by subscription. In 1893 a resolution was passed at a public meeting in favour of using Eastwood House as a museum and art gallery. The museum remained there for over fifty years, but it was eventually decided to move it to Cliffe Castle. Eastwood House became Victoria Hall and is now used as a leisure centre and venue for social events, including performances by Keighley Amateur Operatic and Dramatic Society.

In April 1869, an application was made by the commissioners to build baths and wash-houses in Albert Street but a resolution was passed to defer the scheme for 12 months. The battle of the pro-bathites and anti-bathites continued for another six years, until 1875 and on 4 March 1876 the baths were opened. It was realised how important they were and in 1914 a large new swimming pool was constructed. Improvements were made over the years and other facilities were introduced, including slipper and Turkish baths and various remedial treatments including ultra-violet ray and radiant heat. In winter the pool was covered and was used for dances and other social events. In the 1980s it was realised that the facilities were out of date and a new swimming pool was required, so it was decided to extend the leisure centre in Victoria Park to include one. The pool was opened in 1989 at a cost of £3 million and the old baths were closed. What to do with the old listed building, had been a problem for a number of years, but it has now been converted into houses, retaining the original façade.

On 1 May 1874 a public meeting was convened by the chairman of the Local Board and it was decided that a hospital should be established in the town. Until then, there was no ambulance service nor hospital for accidents or operations and the nearest one was in Bradford. A house was rented in the Highfield Lane area, at a rent of £75 a year and the cottage hospital was opened for use in 1876, with eight beds, using the kitchen table for operations. The hospital was financed mainly by voluntary contributions, but a valuable source of income was from the Friendly Society's annual galas, which were started in 1877. In 1898, the foundation stone was laid for a new hospital, with 35 beds and an administrative block, at a cost of £15,000. The name of the hospital was changed in 1904, to Victoria Hospital, in recognition of the Queen's Jubilee. The hospital continued to expand and develop, until it was decided, along with St John's and Morton Banks hospitals, that they should close and be replaced by Airedale General Hospital at nearby Eastburn. The patients were transferred on 5 May 1970 and the new hospital was officially opened on 11 December 1970 by the Prince of Wales. It cost £5½ million and serves Keighley, Bingley, Skipton and Settle areas, having a total of 643 beds.

Keighley's main street, until the end of the 19th century, was North Street, which was laid out in 1786, but it was not until the 1880s that it began to resemble the street we know today, when it was widened and large imposing buildings began to be built. Cavendish Street was built about the same time and the canopies over the shops were added later and this was the smart shopping area for many years. In the 1960s, like many other towns at that time, the old streets in the centre were demolished and it was developed as a shopping precinct. This was done in phases, so that the old shops could move into the new area as it was completed. This area is now completely under cover and is traffic free. The market was also replaced at this time, from the open air market to a new covered one, which is more convenient but does not have the same character.

In 1899 Andrew Carnegie, the multi-millionaire industrialist, offered £10,000 for a library in Keighley. He was born in Dunfermline and had made his millions in steel in America. When he met Sir Swire Smith, the Keighley educationalist, at a party in Scotland, he offered him the money, provided the town would donate a site and adopt the Libraries Act to provide a service. The library was opened on 20 August 1904, by the Duke of Devonshire and became the first Carnegie library in England. The nucleus of 13,000 books came from the Mechanics' Institute library, as the donation from Mr. Carnegie was for the building only. The services of the library continued to expand to include a reference library in 1912 and a juvenile library in 1929. It was decided that the library could expand no further in the present building and an extension should be built, to include a children's library and a lecture hall. This was opened in March 1961 by the mayor, Alderman J.S. Bell. Later the children's library returned to its original location in the main library, due to the rising costs of running a separate department. Later the lending library was modernised and fitted out with carpets, a suspended ceiling and all new fixtures and fittings. Part of the large reading room, which was superfluous, was added to the lending library. This modernisation was opened by Mrs. Margaret Thatcher, who was then Secretary of State for Education and Science, in July 1972. In 1974, as part of local government re-organisation, Keighley Central Library became part of Bradford Libraries.

The Hippodrome or Queen's Theatre, as it was originally called, was opened on 27 March 1880, by Abraham Kershaw and was made of wood. It was built on a site now occupied by the multi-storey car park, next to the bus station. On 3 May 1889 it was closed for re-building and was virtually demolished and replaced with a stone-fronted building with a slate roof, and was re-opened on 30 August of the same year. The theatre underwent many changes during this period and a new Queen's Theatre was opened on 3 February 1900. The 1930s was a period of decline nationally for theatres but the Hippodrome managed to carry on for another 20 years, until it was officially closed on 11 August 1956. It was re-opened, for a final performance by Keighley Operatic and Dramatic Society, in November of that year. Demolition began in 1961; the land being used to extend the bus station and to build a multi-storey car park. Famous artists that have appeared at the Hippodrome include Charlie Chaplin, Gracie Fields, Max Miller, George Formby and a young Shirley Bassey, who appeared there in the 1950s before she was famous.

The cinema came to Keighley as early as 1898, when Harry Bamforth of Holmefirth, presented a series of short subjects, at the 'Cons' or 'Conversazione'. After that, the town was visited by various touring cinematograph shows until 1909, when the Russell Street Cinema opened, followed by the Theatre De Luxe in Market Street the following year. These were followed in quick succession by the Palace in Cavendish Street (1910), Oxford Hall (1911), the Cozy Corner (1912) and the Picture House (1913). The Regent Cinema did not open until 1920 and the Ritz, which was the most luxurious, until 1938. During the 1950s the town boasted a total of six cinemas but, with the introduction of bingo, they gradually closed, including the Ritz, which became a bingo hall in 1974. The only cinema which has tried to keep going, is the Picture House, which has re-opened a few times and has had its latest grand re-opening in July 1996 and the hope is that it will remain open and keep the cinema tradition going in Keighley.

Sport in Keighley goes back a long way and it is said that cricket has been played in the town since 1820 but unfortunately no record exists of any club established about that time. The Keighley Cricket Club was started on 12 April 1848, when J.W. Sharpe sent out invitations to meet at the *Devonshire Arms Inn* at seven o'clock. A committee was appointed 'to look out for a field and see that two pairs of bats and balls, wickets and bails be ordered from Edward Heaton, ironmonger.' A ground was found in Dalton Lane, at an annual fee of £5, and the club remained there until 1869, when it moved to Lawkholme, where it has remained ever since. Keighley cricketers who have played for England include F.E. Woolley, J.W. Hearne and Schofield Haigh.

Rugby League in Keighley started in October 1876 on a field in Lawkholme owned by E. Holmes, but moved to Dalton Lane two years later. It was not until 1885 that they amalgamated with Keighley Cricket Club, who supplied them with a ready-made ground at Lawkholme. It still remains the home of rugby today, after a difficult period in the 1920s, when apathy brought a threat of closure. In the 1930s, the club flourished and made its only appearance at the Rugby League Challenge Cup final at Wembley in May 1937, when 16 special trains left Keighley taking 9,000 supporters to the game. It was estimated that there were 15,000 supporters at the final, which Keighley lost to Widnes 18-5. Keighley has had many excellent players, including Harry Myers, who was captain for 10 years but who died tragically after a game at Dewsbury in 1906. Others included Ted Spillane, Hal Jones, Geoff Crewdson and the only local-born player to represent Great Britain in a Test match, Terry Hollindrake, who was sold to Hull in October 1960. In recent years, the team has developed a new image and is now called the Cougars and have done a lot of good work for the youth of the town.

Another sport to flourish in Keighley was boxing, which was boosted by the efforts of one man over a 20-year period. He was Harold Beckett, who trained Keighley's professional boxers between 1928 and 1948 and was known as Keighley's Mr. Boxing. This sport is no longer popular in the town.

Other well-known local sporting personalities include the late Trevor Hockey, who started his career with Bradford City football club and went on to play for Wales, Steeton's Kendall Mellor, the cross-Channel swimmer who died in 1989, and Dr. Mike Jones, the white-water canoeist, who was tragically killed in the Himalayas near K2 in 1978.

The town has had its fair share of 'characters', who were to be found on the streets, trying to earn a meagre living and were not unusual in any town in the early part of this century. One of the best known Keighley characters was 'Freddie Gramophone' Butterfield. He had a gramophone mounted on a cart and played to theatre and cinema queues. He also visited big houses in the town. His rivals were Tingalary Tommy, who played a barrel-organ and John Thomas (Bradley), who played a gramophone mounted on a pram. Emily Matchbox used to sing in the street for a few pennies and sold newspapers. She lived with Joe Pump, who accompanied her on the concertina and also sold firewood. Quite a number of 'characters' sold food in the street; usually roast potatoes, chestnuts or hot peas. The best known of these was 'Spud Mick', whose proper name was Michael Macdonald. He had a marvellous shining roast potato machine at the bottom of Cavendish Street and sold three potatoes for a penny. The list is endless but one character who cannot be ignored was 'Old Three Laps', who was christened William Sharp. He got his name from his penny-pinching ways, for when his tailor said there was not enough material for a suit, he said, 'then mak' it wi' three laps'. When he was to be married, the fathers could not agree on the marriage settlement and on the wedding day Mary Smith, his bride-to-be, did not arrive for the ceremony. Shortly afterwards, he took to his bed and stayed there for the next 49 years, until he died on 7 March 1856. He is buried in Keighley Parish churchyard.

Keighley is very much a multi-cultural community, with the Asian population developing its own cultural and religious centres, including a purpose-built mosque, between Bradford Street and Emily Street. The work began in October 1974 and cost about £40,000 and was the first custom-built mosque in Yorkshire and only the third in England.

The industrial and economic development of the town will depend on its transport system. At the present time, the main artery is the Aire Valley Trunk Road, which has progressed from Kildwick to Crossflatts but has been held up by government spending restriction. This will not ease the traffic problem in the area, until it is linked with the motorway systems. The other important scheme is the electrification of the railway in the Aire Valley, which makes a much more efficient and cleaner passenger and freight system and this has now been completed.

Keighley has proved to be a progressive and forward looking town and this collection of photographs shows many of the changes that have taken place over the years.

EARLY KEIGHLEY

1 Keighley in 1848. The view is taken from a drawing looking west, with the river Worth in the foreground. The road climbing the hill is Highfield Lane, which is now a densely populated area. It can be seen at this early date that Keighley was becoming an industrial town with quite a few mills. The other building of note is the parish church, which is to the left of centre.

2 Cornmill Bridge in 1820 from a drawing by John Bradley (1787-1844). The bridge which spanned the North Beck was named after the cornmill which stood at the junction of Oakworth Road and Mill Street. It was demolished when the new road was built, joining Oakworth Road and High Street, in the late 1930s, which involved building a new culvert to cover the beck through the centre of town.

3 'Mr. Craven's Walk Mill', 1 August 1820 from a drawing by John Bradley. In 1783, John Craven went into partnership, to acquire Walk Mill. This partnership continued until 1822, when the mill became the sole property of the Craven family. The mill began spinning by water power about 1812. They were one of the first to introduce power loom weaving, soon after looms were first produced in Keighley in 1834.

4 River Aire from Thwaites Lane, 27 August 1820, also from a painting by the artist John Bradley. The view is of the Aire Valley looking north, with the old Stockbridge crossing the river Aire on the right of the painting. At this time the artist also produced similar works of other parts of the town.

BUYING AND SELLING

5 Gott and Butterfield's hardware shop in the Royal Arcade, Low Street, which closed in 1983. This was a shop in the old tradition which appeared to sell everything and, if they did not stock what you required, they could always get it for you. William Gott started his business in 1890, taking Frank Butterfield into partnership with him in 1910.

6 Mrs. Harriet Shackleton had a stall which was made of old wooden boxes and plied her trade in Cooke Lane. She sold vegetables and flowers until the mid-1960s and was one of the last street traders in Keighley.

7 *(above)* The old market from Market Street, June 1971. The market charter dates from 1305, when it was granted to Henry Kighley by Edward I. It was held on Church Green until November 1833, when it moved to its present permanent site off Low Street and took trading off the streets.

8 *(below)* One of the wooden shops on the side of the Corporation builder's yard, which was eventually replaced by the Town Hall Square. This was the Cavendish Cycle Works, facing Cavendish Street, owned by Mr. W.H. Senior, who can be seen in the doorway.

9 *(top right)* Industrial Co-operative Society, fish and fruit department, *c.*1920, which advertised 'fresh fish from all ports, poultry and game, fruit and vegetables from our own growers and wreaths and bouquets supplied at short notice'. The Co-operative Society started in Keighley on 9 October 1860, when a meeting was held in the Turkish Bath Rooms, in the old market. The first shop was opened in Church Green.

10 *(bottom right)* Spud Mick (Michael Macdonald) and his son Tom. They sold hot roast potatoes from their brightly polished machine, outside the railings of the railway yard at the bottom of Cavendish Street, between the wars. He was one of the many characters who could be found on the streets, trying to earn a living about this time.

CHURCH AND CHAPEL

11 Keighley Parish Church, which survived until 1805 and was built in the 12th century. This small church was replaced by an inferior building which had in turn to be replaced in 1848 by the church which stands at the end of North Street today.

12 The interior of the present parish church of St Andrew, prior to the removal of the galleries over the two side aisles in 1931. The foundation stone was laid by Frederick Greenwood, who was a principal subscriber and the church was consecrated on 11 August 1848 by the Bishop of Ripon.

13 The parish church, which was built from designs by R.D. Chantrell F.S.A. at a cost of £7,000 and was raised by subscription. It is now called the Shared Church, as it is used by Methodists as well as Anglicans.

14 Keighley Salvation Army Silver Band, *c*.1920. The history of the Salvation Army in Keighley goes back to 18 December 1881, when a Major Cadman came to speak to a crowd in the market. On 21 June 1882, the colours were presented to the newly-formed Corps, by the founder, General William Booth.

15 The Friends' Meeting House in Mill Street in 1932. It is generally accepted that the premises were built in 1690 but the date over the door is 1709. There was a small library of books which illustrated the principals of Quakerism and also a small burial ground attached to the chapel.

16 Interior of Temple Street Methodist Church, late 19th century. The chapel was built in 1846 and had seating for about 1,650. Because of diminishing congregations it was no longer required and it is now used as a mosque.

17 Interior of Wesley Place chapel. This was the third Wesley Place chapel, which was opened on Friday 29 November 1867. Its predecessor had to be demolished in May 1865 when the Worth Valley Railway undermined its foundations, as a tunnel was driven under the road. Part of the rebuilding costs was covered by the railway company, after four years of negotiations.

18 Spencer Street Congregational Sunday School, which belonged to Devonshire Street Chapel. It was used as an auxiliary military hospital by the Keighley Corps of the St John Ambulance Brigade during the First World War.

CIVIC AFFAIRS

19 Coronation celebrations of Edward VII. Dignitaries entered the parish church on 9 August 1902, with a policeman checking the crowds. After the adoption of the loyal address by the town council, the procession to the parish church was led by the band of 3rd Volunteer Battalion of the West Riding Regiment. The celebrations lasted all day and included children's tea parties, a procession of historic tableaux and a gala. The day finished with fireworks and bonfires.

20 Coronation celebrations for Edward VII, which included the laying of the memorial stone for the public library. The view up Albert Street from North Street shows the scaffolding for the new public library, which was opened in 1904.

21 Opening of Laycock Institute on 29 October 1927, by Mr. W.A. Brigg. Earlier the residents of the village, which is about a mile west of Keighley, approached Sir Abe Bailey, the millionaire, who gave them half the money they required to build the institute. The remainder they raised themselves in six months and in June 1927 the foundation stones were laid.

22 Members of the Keighley town council in 1890-93. In the middle row, second left, is Alderman Benjamin Septimus Brigg, who was Keighley's first mayor in 1882. Next to him is Richard Longden Hattersley, who was the second mayor in 1883-4. Next is Alderman Ira Ickringill, who was mayor at the time the photograph was taken.

23 The opening of the Municipal Electricity Works in Coney Lane by the mayor Henry C. Longsdon, the mayoress and other officials, on 15 June 1901. The party had been at the annual gala and afterwards their carriages stopped in Cavendish Street. The mayoress switched on the electric street lamps for the first time and then the party went to the electricity works.

24 The opening of the Lower Laithe reservoir, at Sladen Valley, Stanbury by the Earl of Hartington, 11 August 1925. The proceedings started with a luncheon in the Town Hall provided by the chairman of the Waterworks Committee, Ald. W.A. Brigg. The official party then went up to Sladen Valley, which is five miles west of Keighley.

25 General view of the opening of the Lower Laithe reservoir in 1925. The ceremony took place around the valve tower in the middle distance and, after various presentations had been made, afternoon tea was provided in the marquee, on the right of the photograph.

26   The Mechanics' Institute clock which was officially started on 30 June 1892. The clock was donated by Mr. Prince Smith in memory of his father. When the building originally opened in September 1870, the tower was much lower and did not have a clock.

27   Eastwood estate purchase, luncheon party, 30 October 1891. Twenty-one acres of land and Eastwood House were bought for £8,500 and renamed Victoria Park. After the official signing of the deeds, a party of councillors proceeded in carriages to the park and after various ceremonies the mayor, Ira Ickringill, provided a luncheon. The house was opened as a museum in 1899.

28 Unveiling of the war memorial, 7 December 1924 by Lt. Gen. Sir Charles Harrington, GBE, KCB, DSO. The memorial is 35 feet high and is surmounted by a nine foot bronze female figure bearing a wreath in one hand and a palm branch in the other. Many of the people in the large crowd were relatives of the fallen and these made an endless stream to the memorial to lay their tributes.

EARNING A LIVING

29 King's brewery, Cooke Lane, *c.*1958, just before it closed down. It owned the *Eastwood Tavern*, the *Beaumont Arms* and *The Globe*. The head of the firm was Mr. Aaron King, of Tarn House, Keighley, who died on 28 March 1914, aged 80. Originally he came from a Quaker family in Cowling and his grandfather was imprisoned in York Castle, for refusing to pay tithes, in 1785.

30 Russell Street cattle fair in the early 1900s. Fred Burrows, who was born about 1875 and apprenticed at Hird's barber's shop on Cornmill Bridge, remembered the cattle fairs, held in March and September. He said the cattle stood in Bridge Street, Old Mill Street, Chapel Lane, Temple Street and Russell Street. Horses were by the *Ship Inn* and pigs on one side of Church Street. When the fair was over the fire brigade hosed down the streets.

31 Dalton Mills were rebuilt by the Craven family between 1866 and about 1890. Originally there was a small water-powered cotton spinning mill on the site, built about 1790 and known as Strong Close Mill. The mill complex was one of the largest in Keighley and the engines that ran it were reputed to be the largest in the world. Today the buildings are almost empty and plans are in progress to split them into smaller units.

32 The workforce of William Laycock and Sons. Textile leather manufacturers, founded in 1847, they occupied an old-fashioned building at the junction of Queen Street and Bow Street between 1860 and 1961. As the central area development scheme progressed, they were obliged to move to Beta works at Ingrow in May 1961, which proved to be a much better site.

33 Chapel Lane coopery, 1926. The cooper was working in very dilapidated premises, with crumbling roof and broken windows. It is an example of a dying art, as most barrels are now no longer made of wood. This was just one of the many trades carried out in the town, around the turn of the century.

34 National Shell Factory, 1915-18. Fully equipped on 15 November 1915, the women employees worked two shifts of almost 12 hours. The heavy metal bars in the foreground were cut and drilled out to make the shell cases and the finished cases can be seen on the carts.

EDUCATION

35 Drake and Tonson School, Keighley, Preparatory Department, October 1923. Denis Winston Healey, whose father was principal of the Technical College, is fifth from the right in the second row back. He went on to complete his education at Bradford Grammar School and Balliol College, Oxford, before reaching the dizzy heights of Chancellor of the Exchequer and, later, deputy leader of the Labour Party.

36 The Mechanics' Institute before the clock tower was built, in 1892. The foundations of the Temperance Hall, which opened in 1896, can be seen in position on the left of Albert Street. The main hall was used for concerts and had seating for 800 people. There was a smaller hall which accommodated 350 and a number of small rooms, which were used for meetings. Today it is used as a bingo hall.

37 The Mechanics' Institute was opened in 1835 at the corner of North Street and Bow Street. This building was used until 1870, when the new Mechanics' Institute was opened at the top of Cavendish Street. The Yorkshire Penny Bank occupied the old building from 1893 until it was demolished in 1970.

38 Oakbank House, the former home of the Haggas family, with the foundations of the new Boys' Grammar School, being built on the site, March 1962. The school had to move after the disastrous fire at the Mechanics' Institute and was re-opened in 1964. It later became a co-educational comprehensive school and is now called Oakbank School.

39 Andrew Carnegie, multi-millionaire (left centre), probably in September 1900, when he received the Freedom of the Borough, in recognition of providing the town with the first Carnegie library in England. Also in the photograph are Alfred Adams, member of the Technical School council, Denis Barrett, Head of the Technical School, Mrs. Carnegie, Sir Swire Smith, Trustee of the Mechanics' Institute and Augustus Spencer (a local man), principal at the Royal College of Art in London.

40 Memorial stone of the public library, laid by Sir Swire Smith on the coronation day of King Edward VII, 9 August 1902. The library was opened on 20 August 1904 by the Duke of Devonshire.

41 Keighley library reading room, 28 February 1971. The following year this spacious area was used to extend the lending library which was becoming cramped and in need of modernisation.

42 John Drake's Free Grammar School in Cooke Lane, the corner stones of which were laid on 20 August 1716. This building was used until 1854. The School moved again, into the ill-fated Mechanics' Institute in 1872 until March 1962, when it was burnt down.

43 Ald. W.A. Brigg laying one of the foundation stones for the new Girls' Grammar School at Utley on 17 July 1931. The 16-acre site was purchased from the Cliffe Castle estate and the school was officially opened by Lord Halifax in January 1934.

44 Braithwaite Open Air School for delicate children opened on 10 September 1929 by Sir Charles Trevelyan. A bus was provided to take the children to school and they were given breakfast on arrival.

45 The extension to the Technical College making good progress, from North Street, 20 November 1967. The building was not opened until 1970 and incorporated a new town-centre clock. Most of the teaching was done in the new building, which included typing rooms with office furniture and a motor mechanics area designed like a garage bay. The administration was done mainly in the 1957 extension on the right.

KEIGHLEY AT WAR

46 A two-ton Lacre lorry fitted with coal gas container by G.L. Greenwood and Company, wholesale druggists, outside the company's private filling station in 1918. Because of the German blockade, at the start of the First World War, there was a rush to obtain home-produced fuel and soon gas containers and conversion kits were readily available.

47 The enrolment of Eddie Paynter, the England, Lancashire and Keighley cricketer, as a member of the Stickers Club, July 1940. Membership was 1d.; members were given a badge and were pledged to 'stick it' at all costs, whatever the enemy might do. They also promised to obey the government's instructions and always wear the badge.

48 Keighley War Weapons Week, from 30 November to 7 December 1940, had displays in various parts of the town, to raise money for the war effort. These included tanks, a Messerschmitt in the town hall square and war photographs by Yorkshire newspapers. On the first day, there was a parade of military, civil defence, the Home Guard and other organisations from Lund Park and the salute was taken at Bridge Street by Sir Noel Curtis-Benett.

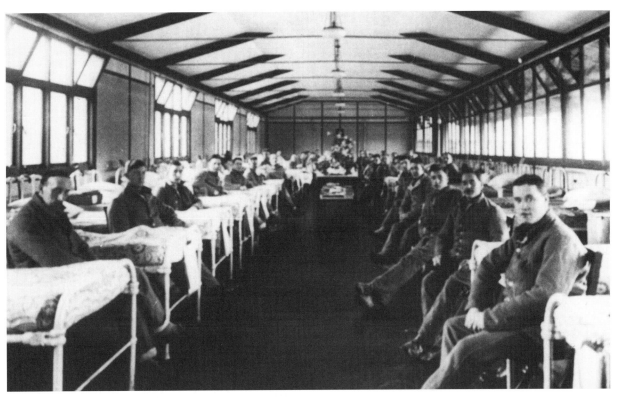

49 Morton Banks Military Hospital, 1917— one of the 12 wards that made up the complex during the First World War. The hospital stood in its own grounds, covering an area of some ten acres and was originally the Keighley and Bingley Fever Hospital. The military hospital was closed on 3 June 1919 and the cases that were left were transferred to Huddersfield.

50 Band Concert at Morton Banks Military Hospital, 5 September 1916. This hospital, which was two miles from the centre of Keighley, was used as a military hospital during the First World War and was re-opened on 18 July 1916 by the mayor; Ald. W.A. Brigg. It provided about six hundred beds and was accepted on behalf of the War Office by Surgeon-General Bedford of Northern Command.

51 Arrival of the first convoy of 30 wounded soldiers at Spencer Street Sunday School, which was being used as an auxiliary military hospital, on 6 May 1915. They were brought in from Leeds in 10 motor cars and one motor ambulance.

52 6th Battalion West Riding Volunteers' flag day, 23 September 1916. The photograph depicts a field dressing station which was erected as near to the firing line as possible, although the members do not seem to be taking it too seriously. The procession made a four-mile tour of the town, with a plea for more men to enlist.

53 6th Battalion West Riding Volunteers' flag day in aid of corps funds, 23 September 1916. There were many tableaux depicting every aspect of war. The most interesting item was a German field gun which had been captured and was escorted by a body of volunteers with rifles and fixed bayonets. Five hundred men took part, including a number of wounded from the hospitals.

54 German prisoners of war at a comrade's funeral at Morton Cemetery on 3 March 1919. In the great influenza epidemic which swept the country at the end of the First World War, 42 Germans died from the camp for officers at Skipton and were buried at Morton. Their remains were later removed to a German military cemetery at Cannock in Staffordshire.

55 War savings effort, March 1918. Scouting biplane displayed on the Town Hall Square for Keighley's submarine week. The campaign was aimed at providing enough money, by the purchase of war bonds and certificates, for Keighley to provide a submarine for the war effort. The children of the town who had bought a certificate, during the week, were given a ticket to inspect the biplane.

56 Dalton Mills were decorated to celebrate the end of the First World War. Within a short time of receiving the news of the signing of the armistice, flags were hoisted on public buildings and factories. Schoolchildren dashed home for their flags, which they had obtained in readiness for the great day, and were given a half-day holiday. Most work-people were given the afternoon off with pay and crowds paraded the streets.

57 Home Guard practising, Second World War. Formed in 1940 as the Local Defence Force, they did very little rifle practice, in their early days, as rifles were in short supply. In August 1941, in anticipation of an invasion, an exercise was carried out, one Sunday morning, and 'enemy agents were rounded up before they could gain vital information and there was fierce street fighting in busy parts of the town'.

KEIGHLEY'S CHANGING FACE

58 The Mechanics' Institute was gutted by fire on 3 March 1962. This building was used for the town's most important civic and social functions and these had to be transferred to Victoria Hall. The shell of the burnt out hall remained for another five years, before it was replaced with an extension to the Technical College.

59 The old packhorse bridge, which was better known as Quebec Bridge, from Westgate *c.*1900. It was demolished in June 1934 and spanned the North Beck for a great many years, although there is no record of its exact age. The parish church can be seen in the distance.

60 Pinfold slum clearance, looking towards the parish church, with the cornmill in the middle distance and Quebec Bridge in the foreground.

61 *(above)* Pinfold slum clearance in the early 1930s. Looking towards Oakworth Road with Springfield Mill rising out of the mist. The photograph is taken from Mill Street with Quebec Bridge still standing in the middle distance.

62 *(top right)* Demolition of a cornmill chimney, 20 July 1934. A large crowd of about three thousand watched as the 80-foot-high chimney fell, which had been a landmark in the town since the 18th century. It is probably the mill mentioned by Miles Gale in 1721, as the King's Mill, which was 'nigh the Town'. The cornmill itself was demolished a year later.

63 *(bottom right)* Demolition of the clock tower of the Mechanics' Institute, 27 April 1966. This was the inevitable result of the fire in 1962, when the shell was left for more than three years, before deciding to build an extension to the college.

64 Demolition of the old market, looking towards Market Street, 13 August 1971. The new covered market was built with the main entrance in Low Street and opened the same year. The hall accommodates a total of 64 stalls and is a far cry from the days when the public had to avoid a leaking roof and puddles on a wet day.

65 Britannia Hall, Market Street, March 1968. Built by the New Britannia Lodge of Oddfellows in 1853, it was used by the Thespian Society who performed Shakespeare and other dramas. Later it became known as Kershaw's Theatre of Varieties. This was before Abraham Kershaw opened the Queen's Theatre in Townfield Gate.

66 Devonshire Street Congregational Church demolition, 30 October 1964. Its foundation stone was laid in 1855 and a block of offices was built on the site. In the background can be seen the Mechanics' Institute, the public library and the police station.

PEOPLE AND PLACES

67 James Leach, whose diary between 1848 and 1853, during his time as a night watchman, graphically describes the seamier side of life in the town, which included all kinds of petty crimes such as drunken brawls, vandalism and prostitution.

68 The unusual memorial stone of James Leach in the town cemetery at Utley. He died in 1893 aged 79 and, apart from being a night watchman and keeping a diary, he led a very active life in service of the town, as can be seen from the gravestone.

69 Henry Isaac Butterfield, textile manufacturer and member of Butterfield Brothers, a company founded by John Butterfield in the early 1800s. Henry was born on 15 February 1818 and was responsible for the rebuilding of Cliffe Hall and renaming it Cliffe Castle, which he filled with valuable paintings and antiques. He died on 11 February 1912.

70 John Farrish, founder member of Keighley Mechanics' Institute. He invited William Dixon, John Haigh and John Bradley to his house at Upper Green, in January 1825. The outcome of this meeting was the formation of a 'society for mutual instruction, and to establish a library for the purpose'.

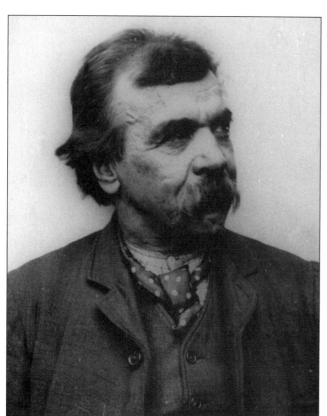

71 'Bill o' th Hoylus End', born 22 March 1836 and christened William Wright, was a dialect poet, who wrote about local events in the town. He is most remembered for his 'History o' Haworth Railway'. He was also the compiler of a 'Howorth, Cowenheead, and Bogthorn Almenak.' He died in 1897.

72 Timmy Feather outside his cottage at Buckley Green, Stanbury. He was born on 20 January 1825 and died on 30 November 1910. He was the last handloom weaver in Keighley and his loom is preserved in Cliffe Castle Museum as a record of a bygone age.

73 Martha Cooke, who kept the *Black Horse* public house in Low Street, was the Keighley postmistress between 1785 and 1833. She was the daughter of the first postmistress, a Mrs. Irvin. The family ran the post office service in the town for a total of 127 years.

74 Netherwood House built on the site occupied by Cliffe Castle. The house was extended and became known as Cliffe Hall but when Sir Henry Isaac Butterfield succeeded to the estate in the early 1870s, he put his ideas into practice and built Cliffe Castle.

75 Cliffe Castle as Henry Isaac Butterfield built it, between 1875 and 1883, showing the towers and turrets which elevated it to the title of castle. Today many of these architectural features have been removed due to dry rot and the building now houses the town's museum.

76 Oakworth House, the magnificent home of Sir Isaac Holden, in the centre of the village of Oakworth. It was built in 1875 to replace the original family home and a year after Sir Isaac died in 1897, the house was put up for auction. Unfortunately nobody could afford to maintain such a large property and it remained empty until 1909, when it was destroyed by fire.

77 Sir John Brigg, M.P. of Kildwick Hall. Sir John was Liberal M.P. for Keighley from 1895 until his death in 1911. He was the second son of John Brigg, worsted manufacture of Guardhouse, and lived on their estate at Calversyke Hill, Keighley. He lived at Kildwick Hall from 1895 to 1911, was made a freeman of the borough in 1897 and knighted in 1909.

PUBLIC HOUSES

78 The *Angel Inn*, Turkey Street, *c*.1930. The upper room was used for stage plays in the mid-19th century. According to William Wright, local writer, 'here there was some local talent, for George Croft played as an amateur, and Randolph Knowles the taylor, along with John Gill … Mrs. Bower, a Keighley resident, was an actress, and Mrs. Reeday … a big women, played as a chambermaid, Mrs. Bower taking the leading parts'.

79 The *Horse and Jockey*, Greengate. This was probably a beershop of ill repute towards the middle of the last century, as John Smith had his licence refused in 1869, because his house was the haunt of prostitutes. It was empty for a number of years after being used as a lodging house and by various firms in the town. It was demolished in 1962.

80 The *Fleece Inn*, Low Street. This was a coaching inn in the early 19th century, when, according to *White's Directory* of 1837, *Alexander* went to Leeds at 6.30a.m. and to Skipton at 7.00p.m. *Tradesman* went to Bradford on Thursdays at 7.30a.m. and *Wonder* went to Halifax on Wednesdays and Saturdays at 7.00a.m. The inn was demolished in 1932, to make way for Marks and Spencer's new store, which opened in 1935.

PUBLIC SERVICES

81 Hillworth Lodge, Oakworth Road, May 1971. This was the workhouse, which opened in 1858 until just before the Second World War, when it was used to house evacuees. In 1948 it became a home for the elderly, and finally closed in January 1971. In spite of its modernisation, the home had the stigma of a workhouse and is now used as part of Keighley College.

82 Keighley fire brigade early this century. The photograph was taken outside the 'new' fire station, which opened in May 1878 and was a converted retort house from the gas works in Coney Lane. The brigade stayed in the premises, until a purpose-built station was opened in Bradford on 29 June 1964, costing £90,000.

83 Keighley police force at the back of Highfield House in 1865, with Sergeant Nichols on the far right. John Gregson is second from the left and was a former watchman under the Improvement Commissioners, before the regular force was introduced.

84 Female ward, Victoria Hospital. This hospital closed on 5 May 1970, when the patients were moved to the new Airedale General Hospital at Eastburn. A site of 32 acres was obtained and work started on the £5.5 million project on 1 September 1965. It serves a population of approximately 155,000 in the Keighley, Bingley, Skipton and Settle area.

85 Victoria Hospital, 28 September 1971. It was named to recognise the Queen's Jubilee in 1904. The cottage hospital was the first opened in 1876 but it was not until 1898 that the foundations for a new Keighley hospital were laid. From 14 November 1915 to 5 April 1919 a wing of the hospital was used for wounded soldiers.

86 Union Infirmary, Fell Lane. The Keighley Guardians purchased land in March 1868 to build the workhouse infirmary, with fever wards 'in case of cholera or other epidemic'. In 1917, it provided beds for the war wounded, until it closed in February 1919. It re-opened to cater for geriatric patients and also had a maternity unit. It closed in August 1970, when the last of its patients were transferred to Airedale Hospital.

ROYAL VISITS

87 A royal visit to Keighley on 29 May 1918. On a tour of the West Riding of Yorkshire, King George V and Queen Mary spent an hour in the town. Thousands lined the streets and the royal party was officially welcomed at the Mechanics' Institute by the mayor, Alderman F.W.L. Butterfield, and the town clerk.

88 Visit of Princess Mary, Vicountess Lascelles on 16 March 1926, to open the X-Ray department at Victoria Hospital. The streets were lined with sightseers, and flags hung from shops and houses in the main streets. There was a guard of honour provided by the 6th Battalion, Duke of Wellington Regiment and the band played the National Anthem. She was accompanied by the mayor, Arthur Smith.

89 Royal visit of Princess Anne, 22 June 1977. The royal party is seen here leaving the helicopter on Holy Family School football field. Accompanying the princess is Brigadier Kenneth Hargreaves, Lord Lieutenant of Yorkshire and Councillor Paul Hockney, Lord Mayor of Bradford and brother of David Hockney, the artist.

SOMEWHERE TO LIVE

90 Oakworth Road with Colne Street on the right, 12 March 1965. This site was eventually cleared in February 1976 and The Oaks home for the elderly was opened by the Lord Mayor of Bradford, Mrs. Doris Birdsall. A year later, in February 1977, on the adjoining land the Oakworth Road Health Centre opened and the area was landscaped.

91 Garden Street in the Eastwood Square area of town, 1901. The worst properties in this area were demolished in the 1930s and a site was eventually cleared for a new fire station, which became operational in June 1964. This replaced the Coney Lane Station and had accommodation for six appliances and a staff of forty-two.

92 Nightingale Street, August 1967, just before it was demolished. The poor condition of the walls can be seen, which were reputed to be coated with a mixture of mud and small pebbles. The walls by this time were porous and crumbling and the properties were known locally as 'muck houses'.

93 Showfield, winter 1868. The attractive entrance to Cliffe Castle is highlighted by a fall of snow and shows off the castellated style. The original gates were taken for salvage during the Second World War, but were replaced by a pair from nearby Sutton Hall, in 1954. The farmer is in the area called Showfield, which is now completely filled with rows of houses.

94 The Ginnel, Westgate in the 19th century. This was an overcrowded part of the town, which was most unhealthy and was demolished in the slum clearance scheme of the 1930s. Amongst these streets there was a total of 17 slaughter houses by 1901, many of which were unfit for the preparation of human food.

95 The Barracks, Westgate. These were originally Damside Mill, which was rebuilt by Betty Hudson in 1802 and taken over by Jonas Greenwood, William and Lister Ellis about 1805. Eventually the mill engine was removed and by about 1820 it was converted into cottages for use by hand combers. The building got its name because of its close resemblance to a soldier's barracks.

96 The Lodging House, West Turkey Street, May 1962. Originally a Baptist chapel, it closed as a lodging house in May 1962, forcing the 72 occupants to seek alternative accommodation. There was also a burial ground attached to the old chapel, which was the site of 68 burials between 1816 and 1865. In December 1964, the bodies were re-buried at the town's main cemetery at Utley.

SPORTS AND PASTIMES

❖

97 Oxford Hall, Oakworth Road, May 1972. The Oxford Hall cinema opened on 20 March 1911, only two years after the first cinema in Russell Street. It closed as a cinema on 13 June 1959 and has carried on as a bingo hall ever since.

98 Motor coaches in Cooke Lane departing for Keighley Feast holidays, *c.*1930. The Feast holiday is still recognised as an official holiday in Keighley but it does not have the same impact it once had. There was a mass exodus and the town seemed deserted for a week. In the 18th century, the Feast was a time for merrymaking and included drinking and bull baiting.

99 Lifeboat Saturday, North Street, 23 August 1902. The public turned out in large numbers and lined the streets for this annual event, as this was something special. The *Tranmore* lifeboat had been hired with a crew from Scarborough and were horse-drawn. The procession was headed by Cowling Temperance Band, who were followed by the mayor and mayoress and other officials. The procession was completed with a tableau of Grace Darling.

100 Parkwood bonfire, to commemorate Queen Victoria's diamond jubilee, 22 June 1897. The event was declared a holiday and peals of bells could be heard from the parish church at frequent intervals. There was a Sunday School procession, which included five bands and 35 Sunday Schools took part. The Parkwood bonfire was a great success, containing 50 tons of material which was still alight the following morning.

101 Keighley rugby league team, Wembley, 8 May 1937. This was the only time that Keighley appeared at the Challenge Cup final. The week before the match, the team had their usual training sessions and extra exercise on Ilkley Moor, with an hour's practice on Wembley Stadium. They lost to Widnes, 18 points to 5.

102 Keighley Cycling Club, *c.*1890. The club started in 1884 with nine members, who met in various wooden huts in the town. By 1897 the club had become so popular it was able to move into permanent three-storey premises in Cavendish Street. Unfortunately the days of cycling have been overtaken by the motor car, but the club still exists purely as a social club.

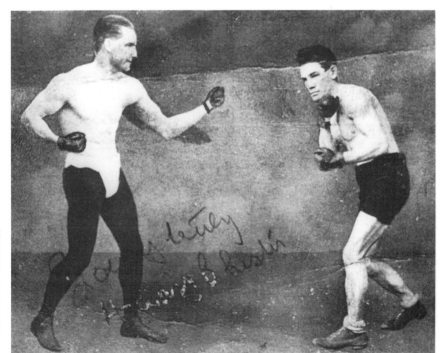

103 Promotion for boxing match between Sapper George Clark and Harry Chester. This event took place in the Baths Hall in December 1920, which was also the venue for dances. The pool was covered, when not used for swimming, and drained. In 1954 the hall was modernised and renamed the Queen's Hall, for the dancing season.

104 Wesley Place Chapel choir, *c.*1907, with the choirmaster Mr. James Hey. The chapel also had a male voice choir and string band whose performances were a major attraction in the area. At this time, the chapel was in its heyday and there were lots of activities taking place including cricket, football, table tennis and gymnastic teams.

105 The Friendly Society's gala procession in Cavendish Street on 17 July 1911. The first gala was in 1877 and has always taken place in Victoria Park or the grounds of Eastwood House, as it was called at that time. The gala is still an important occasion in the Keighley calendar of events.

106 River Aire at Stockbridge on 19 February 1929. This was the first time this century that the river had frozen over to such an extent that it permitted skating on it. At the same time, a special bus service ran from town to Keighley Tarn, which is about a mile away, and hundreds arrived by motor car.

107 Garden party at Kildwick Hall, June 1914, with the mayor of Keighley William Anderton Brigg in the centre of the photograph. He and his twin brother, Dr. J.J. Brigg, a noted local historian, made it their home from 1911 until just before the Second World War.

108 Fancy dress party, probably at Kildwick Hall, at the turn of the century. The owner, William Anderton Brigg, is on the right of the photograph, dressed as Napoleon.

109 Hippodrome Theatre interior, 1956. This was at the time of its closure, before being demolished in 1961. Originally called the Queen's Theatre and opened in 1880, this magnificent building seated 492 in the stalls, 257 in the circle and 400 in the gallery. There were three public bars and the artistes had the use of seven dressing rooms.

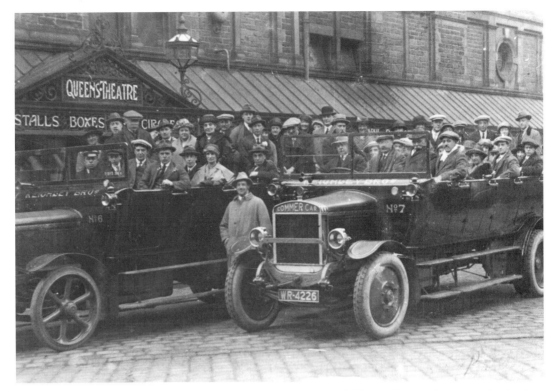

110 'Charabangs' which were owned by Keighley Brothers of Chapel Lane, who were also haulage contractors. They were parked outside the Queen's Theatre at the start of a theatre staff outing in the 1920s.

111 Keighley and District Photographic Association on an outing in the early 1900s. The association was formed on 18 January 1889, when a group of 'persons interested in photography', met 'to consider the advisability of forming a photographic association for the town and district'. In the 1930s the association produced a photographic survey of the town and half the photographs in this book are selected from this collection.

Town Centre

112 Cooke Lane showing the Conservative Club, the Salvation Army Citadel and the bonded warehouse of E. and T. Wall, shortly before they were demolished in 1961, to make way for the new shopping centre. Since 1897 the warehouse casks of wine came from the Mediterranean but, because it was stored under bond, it could not be visited without a customs official being present.

113 Gas showrooms, Cooke Lane, which were opened on 6 May 1902. Initially gas was produced in 1825 for the purpose of street lighting and not until this was accomplished were the Improvement Commissioners allowed to sell gas to the general public. The first gas works were at Low Bridge but moved to Thwaites in 1876.

114 *(above)*　North Street in 1885 with the Mechanics' Institute and the Corporation builder's yard on the left. On the far right, behind the trees is the site of the police station and the public library. This was before the road was widened and horse trams were still in use.

115 *(top right)*　Church Green, looking towards the junction of Low Street and North Street, 1904. The workman are relaying the tramlines for the new electric trams. The public house on the right is the *King's Arms*, which was a coaching inn and one of the oldest public houses in Keighley, being built about 1742. It was demolished in 1966.

116 *(right)*　The fifth home of the Keighley post office in North Street. Impressed by the increased business which James Cooke, the postmaster, had created, the authorities decided to move the post office to larger accommodation, when he retired in 1877. It stayed there until 1891.

117 The sixth home of the Keighley post office at Townfield Gate. It was opened by Mrs. James Cooke on 21 September 1891. The building is now part of the council offices and the post office is now in the new shopping centre.

118 Lawkholme Crescent from Lawkholme Lane, 8 July 1967. Some of the shops which moved into the new shopping centre the following year were in this row. The present bus station offices can be seen on the right of the photograph.

119 Townfield Gate, *c*.1925. Although quite a number of buses can be seen near the area which was to be the bus station, it was not opened until 1940. The building on the right is in the process of being demolished to open up the site to make way for the bus station as it is today.

120 Cavendish Street from East Parade, at about the turn of the century, before the parade of shops was fully developed and the various streets crossing it were closed. Canopies were added later, making the street as it is today. The goods yard on the right was closed in 1961 and a supermarket and car park were built on the site in 1983.

121 The Hippodrome Theatre and the new bus station after its completion in September 1940. The theatre was closed in 1956 and was eventually replaced by the multi-storey car park which opened in June 1970, when the bus station was once again extended.

122 *(left)*   Hanover Street from Cavendish Street, 11 July 1967. As can be seen from some of the shop fronts, demolition of the old street was in progress and soon it would be transformed into an important thoroughfare of the town. This was the south-eastern boundary of the new shopping centre, which was to fight with Cavendish Street for its shopping customers.

123 *(below left)*   Cavendish Street, at the end of the 19th century. The bottleneck, which was caused by the *Queen's Head* on the right and the *Oddfellow's Arms* on the left, was removed by demolishing both public houses. The *Cavendish Hotel* replaced the *Oddfellows Arms* at the junction of Lawkholme Lane in 1900.

124 *(below)*   View from Airedale Works of Sandywood Street with Lund Street and Holker Street running into North Street across the middle of the photograph, in 1898. Devonshire Park can be seen in the distance to the right of the picture.

125 *(above)*   The Cross looking east in 1904. This was so named because of the original location of the market cross outside the *Devonshire Arms*, which is just off the photograph on the right.

126 *(above right)*   Low Street looking west about the turn of the century. This gradually became a narrow, busy street, until part of it was pedestrianised as an experiment for Christmas 1971 and was made permanent in the spring of the following year.

127 *(right)*   Groves Corner at the junction of Cooke Lane and Low Street is a good example of how Low Street looked in the 19th century. These shops were demolished in 1930 to make way for a three-storey block of shops. James Groves, who was the owner of the corner shop, had run the grocery business in the town for 35 years, until his death in 1916.

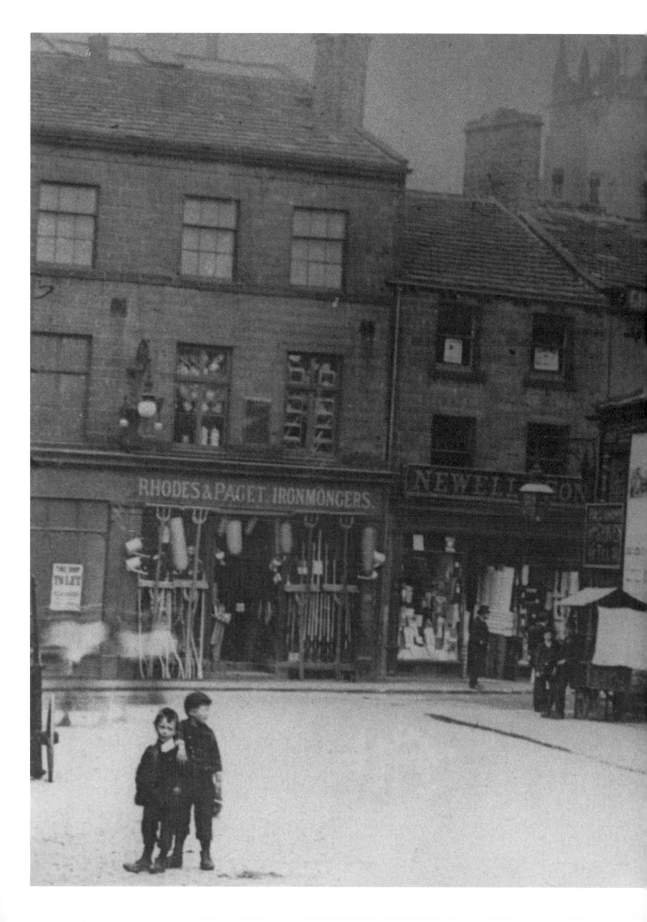

128 Low Street from Cooke Lane in 1900, with the parish church in the distance. The buildings in the centre of the photograph, in Low Street, are much the same today but Cooke Lane was demolished in September 1961 to make way for the new shopping precinct. To mark the completion of the first phase of the project, a commemorative stone was laid on 8 May 1968.

129 North Street in 1893. The houses on the left were on the site of the public library, which opened in 1904. The hoardings and wooden shops on the right of the picture, surrounded the Corporation stone-yard, which was laid out as the Town Hall Square in 1907.

130 Cavendish Street, with its smart shops and imposing buildings, looking east. The central electric light pillars were removed in 1904, with the introduction of the electric tramway system. The Corporation builder's yard and small wooden shops on the right were transformed into the Town Hall Square in November 1907. The war memorial was added much later, in December 1924.

131 Shops in Low Street, 1927. The shop on the left, William Laycock and Sons Limited, was founded in 1847 and moved into its Queen Street factory in 1860. The property in Low Street was used as an office for a number of years until Woolworths took over the site, then moved into the new shopping centre in 1968, when the property was demolished.

132 Coney Lane corner at the junction with Low Street in 1928. The shops were demolished in 1929 and the site was used for the electricity showrooms until they were closed in 1959. It is now the site of the offices of the Inland Revenue and Social Security.

133 *(above)* Shops in Low Street before the alterations of 1927. Note the sign for the Cosy Corner cinema on the end of the shops. The cinema was on the left-hand side of the road down a passage and was known locally as the flea pit. It was amongst the first cinemas in Keighley, opening in 1912.

134 *(top right)* Low Street looking east in 1932. The shop on the left, J. Bottomley & Sons was founded by Mr. Jonas Bottomley in 1866 and they also manufactured a large selection of high-class boiled sweets. The business was so successful, that a large factory was opened in Adelaide Street in 1887. It was famous nationally for its mint rock and lime fruit tablets.

135 *(right)* Sneed's Corner at the junction of North Street and High Street, *c.*1890. John Sneed the druggist's shop is on the corner with Uttley, the milliner's, upstairs. Note the demolition of the old properties on the right of North Street and the style of uniform the police are wearing.

136 *(left)*   North Adelaide Street, 16 August 1967, part of the redevelopment of the town centre to make a new shopping centre. This view looks towards Cavendish Street over the site of Smith Brothers Engineers, showing the Halifax Building Society on the corner. The buildings in Cavendish remain unchanged.

137 *(below left)*   The Town Hall Square *c.*1920 before the erection of the war memorial in the centre. On the far side is the Mechanics' Institute and Cavendish Street United Free Church, which was closed to worship in 1937. The church opened in 1857 and is now the site of the main building of Keighley College.

138 *(below)*   South Street at the junction with Aireworth Street in the 1930s. The *Friendly Inn* on the corner, which is only small, is still there today, as are the other buildings in the row and little has changed, except that the road is no longer cobbled. The large building on the right of the photograph is the cornmill, which was demolished in July 1935.

493/63 Devonshire Park, The Fountain, Keighley

139 Devonshire Park fountain. This fountain was originally on Church Green and was presented to the town by Miss Butterfield of Cliffe Hall in 1869. It was to replace the stocks, which the Temperance Society campaigned to have removed. The fountain was moved to Devonshire Park, to make way for road traffic in 1888.

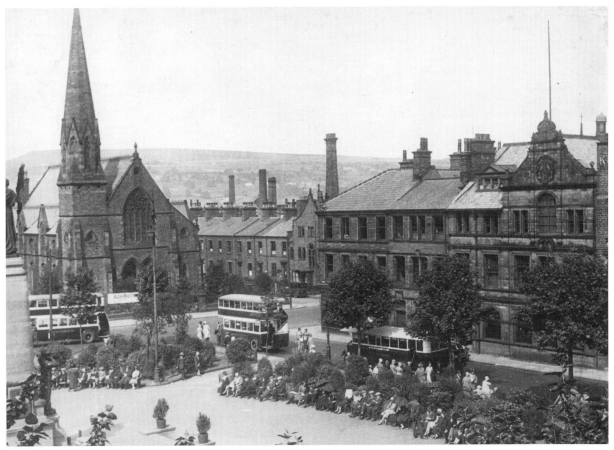

140 The Town Hall Square in summer 1932. The war memorial, which is on the left of the photograph, was unveiled in 1924 and the square was a popular place, where lots of shrubs were planted. The main form of transport was the bus and there is not a car in sight. The only building which is not there today is the Cavendish Street United Free Church but the scene projects a much more relaxed atmosphere.

141 Townfield gate used as a builder's yard. Originally, back in the Middle Ages, the Townfield was common land, which was ploughed by the villagers. It covered an area of about one hundred acres to the north east of the town and the gate was at its most southerly point. The high building in the centre of the photograph is the Hippodrome Theatre.

TRANSPORT

142 The new road at Stockbridge during alterations to replace the old stone bridge in 1929. The new concrete bridge was opened on 4 September 1930 and straightened the road.

143 The first steam wagon of George Hattersley and Sons Ltd., the Keighley loom makers, which was built in Leeds in 1905. These wagons, weighing seven tons each, were used to carry looms and were able to carry four at once at a speed of four miles an hour. The driver is Mr. Sam Hardwick.

144 Re-laying tramlines at the junction of North Street and Cavendish Street, to convert to electrification. This system was opened on 12 October 1904. The tramlines were removed in 1924, when a much cheaper trackless system was introduced.

145 Withdrawal of the Keighley trackless service, 31 August 1932. The last trackless left the Town Hall at 11 o'clock in the evening, with the mayor, Alderman M.P. Cryer, acting as driver and Alderman Albert Smith, chairman of the Tramways Committee, as conductor.

146 The trial run of the new electric tramways car no.1, at the terminus at Ingrow, 16 September 1904. The fare from Utley to Ingrow was less than $1\frac{1}{2}$d. and the manager had a wooden office in the Town Hall Square.

147 The Leeds and Liverpool canal at Riddlesden. The Bingley to Skipton section opened first, on 7 April 1773, when two boats arrived in Skipton laden with coal. The canal is 127 miles long and has 91 locks raising the height to 487 feet above sea level. It no longer carries commercial traffic and since 1972 has been used only by pleasure craft.

148 The last electric tram in Keighley outside the *Roebuck* public house at Utley in October 1924. This was before the introduction of the new trolleybus service the same year and a large workforce can be seen preparing for the new road surface for the changeover.

149 Bradford Road before Station Bridge was built in 1879. The crossing gate had begun to hold up the traffic from Bradford and was a danger to pedestrians. The old station was on the right-hand side of the road, behind Cavendish Street, but was moved to the left-hand side in 1883.

150 The Town Hall livery stables, North Street, which was owned by Joseph Smith. As the site is on a slope the horses climbed up a ramp to their quarters upstairs. The building was converted into the Regent Cinema in 1920 and closed on 6 December 1964 to be used for bingo. It then became a nightclub which changed hands once again in 1996.

151 First electric tram car in Cavendish Street, 12 October 1904. The electrification of the service was officially opened in the afternoon when the mayor, William Clough, accompanied by the mayoress and other members of the council, drove the first tram, which was decorated with flags. On leaving the depot, he steered the car to Bridge Street and then to the Cross, where he climbed to the upper deck and addressed a large crowd.

152 The old Stockbridge, which was built in the 18th century and proved narrow and difficult to negotiate for modern traffic. The photograph was probably taken early this century, as the new bridge opened in 1930. The building in the centre of this photograph was called Ivy Cottage.

153 Aerial view of the new Stockbridge, with the temporary wooden bridge still in use, shortly before it opened in September 1930. The field at the top left of the photograph was part of the East Riddlesden Hall estate and was later sold off as building land for private houses.

154 *(right)*   Accident at Mechanics' Institute in Cavendish Street, 5 April 1938. The three occupants of the car had a lucky escape as it skidded and crashed through the railings, dropping 10 feet into the area of the Mechanics' Institute. The driver, Mr. Wilfred Barber, a hotel proprietor from Morecambe, was with his wife and a friend, neither of whom was injured.

155 *(left)*   Decorated tram on the occasion of the coronation of George V, 22 June 1911. This was just one item in a full programme, which started with cinematograph shows for children. At the end of the day there was a gala in Victoria Park, attended by 25,000 people, but the children's sports at Lawkholme had to be abandoned, as the crowd of 10,000 became unmanageable.

156 *(below left)*   The old railway station was behind the shops of Cavendish Street. The station was built in 1846 and at the beginning of the 1880s it was recognised that better accommodation was required and that the 'ruinous structure' must be replaced. When the line from Thornton to Keighley was built, the new station opened on the other side of Bradford Road in 1883 and the old station was demolished.

157 *(below)*   The station staff at Keighley railway station. The photograph was taken about the turn of the century and includes their policeman and even the station cat who manned the station 24 hours a day. This was the heyday of the rail service around Keighley, which started in 1847 with the old railway station and ended with the Beeching cuts in the 1960s.

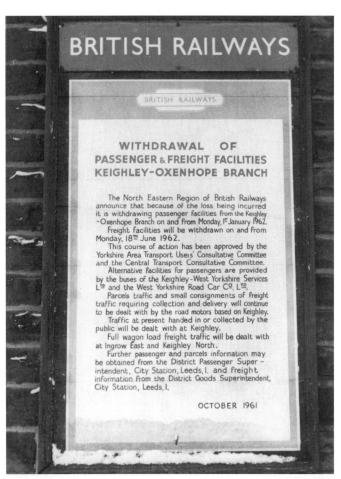

BRITISH RAILWAYS

BRITISH RAILWAYS

WITHDRAWAL OF PASSENGER & FREIGHT FACILITIES KEIGHLEY-OXENHOPE BRANCH

The North Eastern Region of British Railways announce that because of the loss being incurred it is withdrawing passenger facilities from the Keighley -Oxenhope Branch on and from Monday, 1st January 1962.

Freight facilities will be withdrawn on and from Monday, 18th June 1962.

This course of action has been approved by the Yorkshire Area Transport Users' Consultative Committee and the Central Transport Consultative Committee.

Alternative facilities for passengers are provided by the buses of the Keighley-West Yorkshire Services Ltd. and the West Yorkshire Road Car Co. Ltd.

Parcels traffic and small consignments of freight traffic requiring collection and delivery will continue to be dealt with by the road motors based on Keighley.

Traffic at present handed in or collected by the public will be dealt with at Keighley.

Full wagon load freight traffic will be dealt with at Ingrow East and Keighley North.

Further passenger and parcels information may be obtained from the District Passenger Super-intendent, City Station, Leeds, I. and freight information from the District Goods Superintendent, City Station, Leeds, I.

OCTOBER 1961

158 *(left)* Notice, by British Railways, announcing the withdrawal of the Keighley to Oxenhope branch line in October 1961. The passenger service was withdrawn from 1 January 1962 and the freight service from 18 June 1962. It was not until 29 June 1968 that the re-opening 'special' left Keighley, with the Mayor of Keighley, the late Alderman J.H. Waterworth on the footplate, bringing into existence the Keighley and Worth Valley Railway.

159 *(below)* Removal van owned by J. Walker and Son of Aireworth Road, *c.*1920. It was a Sentinel six-ton undertype steam wagon, manufactured by Alley and Maclellan of Glasgow. First going into production in 1906, it was the most popular steam wagon made at this time.

AROUND AND ABOUT

160 Haworth Main Street, *c*.1900. The Brontë village of Haworth, which is about two miles south west of Keighley, has changed little since this photograph was taken. The shops are now aimed at the tourist market and it is crowded with visitors at weekends, but the cobbled street remains the same.

161 Haworth Parsonage, from a pen and ink drawing by William Scruton, was the home of the Brontë family from 1820 to 1861. The Brontë Society was formed in 1893, to preserve Brontë relics in premises over the Yorkshire Penny Bank, in the main street, as the Parsonage and its contents had been sold off. The Parsonage was donated by Sir James Roberts and the Brontë Parsonage Museum opened in 1928.

162 Old Bar House, Bar House Lane, which was used by the Keighley and Kendal Turnpike Trust to collect tolls and was demolished in 1932. This was the route of the old road, by way of Spring Gardens Lane from 1782 until 1825, when the new road from Utley to Hawcliffe was opened.

163 The toll bar house at the bottom of Bar Lane Riddlesden. Tolls were last collected here in 1868 but it was a feature of Stockbridge for about one hundred and fifty years. It was used as a grocer's shop for a period up to 1972, when it was demolished to improve safety on the road, as it was considered one of the main danger spots in the Keighley area.

164 West Riddlesden Hall, *c.*1930. This was the residence of the Maud or de Monhaut family who lived there from about 1450 to 1680, when it became the property of the Leach family by marriage. That family resided there until 1854 when the family line died out on the death of William Leach. It has had various owners since then.

165 Sunnydale, East Morton, which is about two miles east of Keighley, about the turn of the century. The Sunnydale mill produced paper for bank notes and stationery between 1844 and 1878 and was powered by two very large water-wheels. The owner, John Smith, built the row of eight cottages for the workforce and these were occupied until the mid-1940s.

166 View of Sladen Valley on 27 May 1911. Site of the proposed new reservoir for Keighley, which was not opened until 1925. It covers an area of over 31 acres and has a capacity of 281 million gallons.

167 Ingrow Fold, *c*.1913. These 17th-century cottages, about a mile from the town centre, were demolished in 1960 and the barns were removed even earlier. The date carved above the main door was 1663. Note the animal drinking trough in the foreground.

168 Kildwick Hall in the 1930s. A much smaller hall appears to have been on the site as far back as Norman times but the present hall is 17th-century with stone mullioned windows. It stands in about nine acres of land above Kildwick village, with magnificent views of the Aire valley and Keighley which is about four miles away.

169 *(top right)* East Riddlesden Hall in the 1930s. The hall is one mile from Keighley on Bradford Road. It was built largely in the 1640s by the Murgatroyd family but unfortunately the estate belonged to absentee landlords during the 19th century and most of the land was sold off for building. The hall was under threat of demolition in 1934, but it was bought and presented to the National Trust.

170 *(right)* Laverock Hall in the 1930s. Erected in 1641 by Henry and Mary Pighills in the Elizabethan style, and is believed to be on the site of a much older building. The estate is thought to date back to Richard de Haworth around 1320.

171 Scar Top Brewery, Stanbury. Ponden and Watersheddles reservoirs were starting to be built in 1870 and William Heaton decided that a brewery would be a good investment to supply the labour force with plenty of drink. The brewery lasted until 1878, just after work on the reservoirs was completed.

172 Aireworth Ford, 1898. The ford crossed the river Worth from the left of the footbridge to the right-hand bottom corner of the photograph. In 1900 this bridge was replaced by a road bridge, when Aireworth Road was built. On the left behind the wall are the grounds of Aireworth House and, round the next bend, the river Worth joins the river Aire.

173 Ponden Reservoir during construction. This fulfilled a desperate need for water in Keighley and, along with Watersheddles and Blackhill Reservoirs, took eight years to build. They were completed in 1877.

174 Single-decker bus in Braithwaite village main street. The street still exists but the Braithwaite-Laycock by-pass was built in 1938 to avoid the bottleneck. The buildings which make up the street were considered to be of architectural importance in 1977 and it was made a conservation area.

Bibliography

Bancroft, Harry *et al.*, *One Hundred Years 1848-1948* (1948)

Barnett, M. Ratcliff, *Sladen Valley Waterworks* (1925)

Barraclough, F., *A Short History of Keighley Post Office* (1941)

Baumber, Michael L., *From Revival to Regency: A History of Keighley and Haworth 1740-1820* (n.d.)

Baumber, Michael L., *A Pennine Community on the Eve of the Industrial Revolution: Keighley and Haworth between 1660 and 1740* (n.d.)

Brigg, John J., *East Riddlesden Hall* (1936)

Brigg, John J., *The King's Highway in Craven* (1927)

Dewhirst, Ian, *A History of Keighley* (1974)

Gale, Rev. Miles, *The History of the Free School in Kighley* (c.1720)

Hodgson, John, *Textile Manufacture and other Industries in Keighley* (1879)

Hood, J.C.F., *An Account of Keighley Parish Church* (1935)

Keighley, William, *Keighley Past and Present* (1858 and 1879)

Keighley and District Photographic Association, *Keighley Photographic Survey* (n.d.)

Keighley Borough Council, *The Jubilee Book of Keighley* (1932)

Keighley Borough Council, *Public Library Service in Keighley, 1904-1954*

Keighley Community History Group, *Fowk We Remember* (n.d.)

King, J.S., *Keighley Corporation Transport* (1964)

Lawkholme Lane: 100 Years of Rugby (n.d.)

Laycock, John, *History of the Keighley Gas Undertaking, 1825 to 1925* (1925)

Leach, T.M. (comp.), *A History of Keighley West Yorkshire* (1981)

Lock, John, *A Guide to Haworth, the Brontës' Moorland Home* (1956)

Povey, R.O.T., *The History of the Keighley and Worth Valley Railway* (1963)

Recollections of the War Hospital, Keighley, and its Auxilliaries, 1916-19 (n.d.)

Smith, Maurice, *Oakbank History Trail* (1982)

Snowden, Keighley, *The Master Spinner: a Life of Sir Swire Smith, I.L.D., M.P.* (1921)

Thompson, D., *Scar Top Brewery* (1977)

White, William, *Directory and Gazetteer of Leeds, Bradford and the whole of the clothing districts, of the West Riding of Yorkshire* (1847 and 1853)

White, William, *History, Gazetteer and Directory of the West Riding of Yorkshire* (1837)

White, William, *Directory and Topography of the Boroughs of Leeds and Bradford* (1861)

Wilson, E. and Hewitt, R., *A History of Keighley Fire Service* (1986)

Index

Roman numerals refer to pages in the Introduction, and arabic numerals to individual illustrations.